A little

your History

You all very much!

Aunt Bern

XOXO

MW00775016

BY WILLIAM BOEKESTEIN | ILLUSTRATED BY EVAN HUGHES

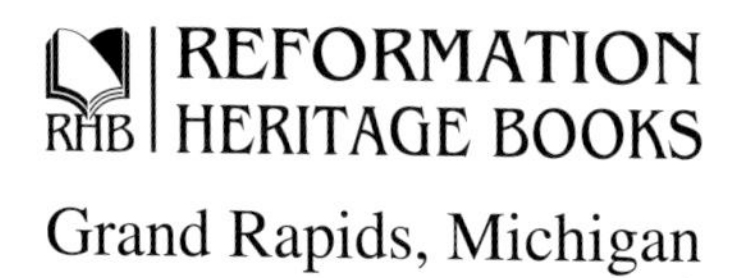

Grand Rapids, Michigan

The Glory of Grace: The Story of the Canons of Dort

Reformation Heritage Books
2965 Leonard St. NE
Grand Rapids, MI 49525
616-977-0889 / Fax 616-285-3246
orders@heritagebooks.org
www.heritagebooks.org

Library of Congress Cataloging-in-Publication Data

Boekestein, William.
The glory of grace : the story of the Canons of Dort / by William Boekestein ; illustrated by Evan Hughes.
pages cm
ISBN 978-1-60178-191-8 (hardcover : alk. paper) 1. Synod of Dort (1618-1619 : Dordrecht, Netherlands). Canones Synodi Dordrechtanae--Juvenile literature. 2. Reformed Church--Creeds--Juvenile literature. I. Hughes, Evan, illustrator. II. Title.
BX9478.B64 2012
238'.42--dc23
2012033043

For additional Reformed literature, both new and used, request a free book list from Reformation Heritage Books at the above regular or e-mail address.

Printed in the United States of America
13 14 15 16 17 18/11 10 9 8 7 6 5 4 3 2

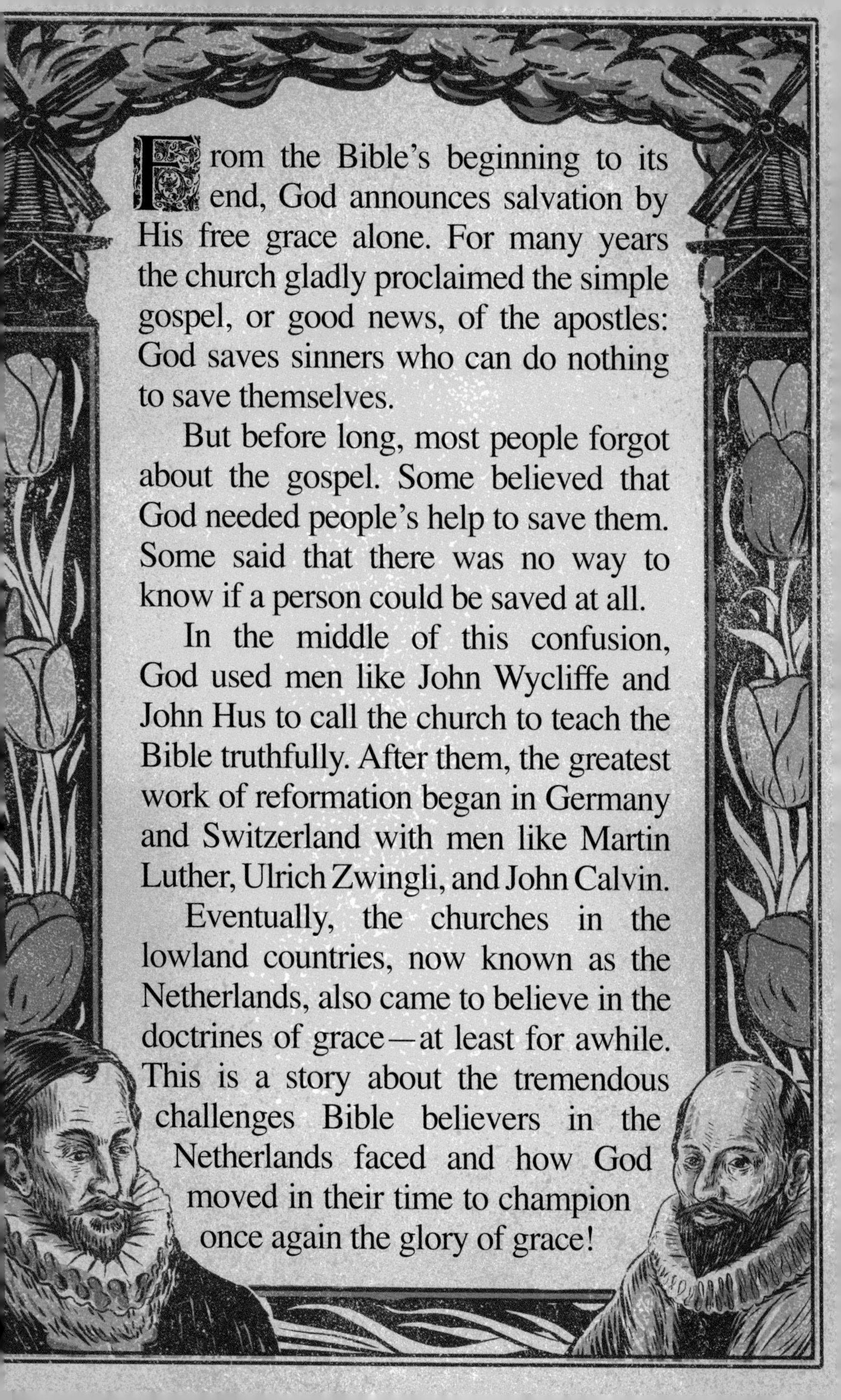

From the Bible's beginning to its end, God announces salvation by His free grace alone. For many years the church gladly proclaimed the simple gospel, or good news, of the apostles: God saves sinners who can do nothing to save themselves.

But before long, most people forgot about the gospel. Some believed that God needed people's help to save them. Some said that there was no way to know if a person could be saved at all.

In the middle of this confusion, God used men like John Wycliffe and John Hus to call the church to teach the Bible truthfully. After them, the greatest work of reformation began in Germany and Switzerland with men like Martin Luther, Ulrich Zwingli, and John Calvin.

Eventually, the churches in the lowland countries, now known as the Netherlands, also came to believe in the doctrines of grace—at least for awhile. This is a story about the tremendous challenges Bible believers in the Netherlands faced and how God moved in their time to champion once again the glory of grace!

Long before Jesus came to earth, the people who lived in the lowlands (today we call them the Dutch) lived in spiritual darkness. Around seven hundred years after Christ's birth, missionaries brought the teachings of the Roman Catholic Church to the lowlands. Many Dutch people believed these teachings, as they would for the next eight hundred years. In 1517, Martin Luther boldly spoke out against some of the Roman Catholic Church's errors. Soon, many Dutch people began to believe the simple gospel message of the reforming church.

But the Catholic Holy Roman Empire that ruled over the Netherlands, first under the Spanish king Charles V and then his son Philip II, would not lose its control without a fight. By the time Martin Luther was buried beneath the Castle Church of Wittenberg in 1546, a terrible persecution called the Spanish Inquisition had begun. Thousands of Dutch Christians were put to death.

Spain

754 British missionary Boniface martyred in Lowlands

1517 Martin Luther posts 95 Theses

1520 Charles V becomes ruler of Netherlands

1500

Empire of Charles V
The Netherlands
1563
Heidelberg Catechism published
1581
Dutch declare independence from Spain
1618-1619
Synod of Dort
1610
Five Points of Arminianism published
1555
Philip II becomes ruler of Netherlands
1567
Guido de Bres martyred
1584
William of Orange killed
1600

By God's grace the Inquisition did not destroy the Reformed church. In fact, many Dutch people began to help the Reformed cause by fighting against Roman Catholic Spain.

One such hero was the Prince of Orange, a wealthy nobleman named William the Silent. Under William's leadership the Spaniards were slowly and painfully pushed back. William was greatly helped by the efforts of the Sea Beggars, a group of fierce sailors who freed several important towns and encouraged the Dutch people to fight for their freedom.

Spain was outraged by William's success. In 1580 Philip declared William an outlaw, offering twenty-five thousand gold coins to the person who would turn him in, a reward he would have to pay four years later.

Despite persecution and war, the Reformed church in the Netherlands grew. The churches knew that in such troubled times they would have to agree on the Bible's main teachings. They already had two confessions, or statements of belief: the Belgic Confession and the Heidelberg Catechism. Both writings unified the church around the Bible's message of salvation through faith alone, in Christ alone, to the glory of God alone. Ministers and elders were required to agree to these truths. In the 1560s, church leaders wrote an agreement called a church order to help them work better as one body.

When the Dutch Republic declared its independence from Spain in 1581, the Reformed faith became the official Dutch religion, and some of the unbiblical ways of worship taught by the Roman Catholic Church were outlawed. In fact, the church and the government became quite closely connected in their joint struggle against Spain.

Arminius

A short time after the Netherlands became independent, the unity and doctrine of the Dutch churches came under attack from several church leaders and their disciples.

The teachings of the British monk Pelagius lived on though he had been dead for more than a thousand years. He taught that people are not born as sinners; they sin only because they follow many bad examples. By following the example of Jesus people can help save themselves. Instead, the Bible says that no one is righteous—not even one.

The ideas of the Dutch scholar Erasmus, who lived at the time of Martin Luther, also shaped the people's opinions. Erasmus had argued against Martin Luther, saying that man's will is free to choose for or against God. Many Dutch pastors followed Erasmus and were removed from their positions for teaching against the doctrines they swore to uphold.

But the greatest challenge to the doctrines of grace came from a man named Jacob Arminius.

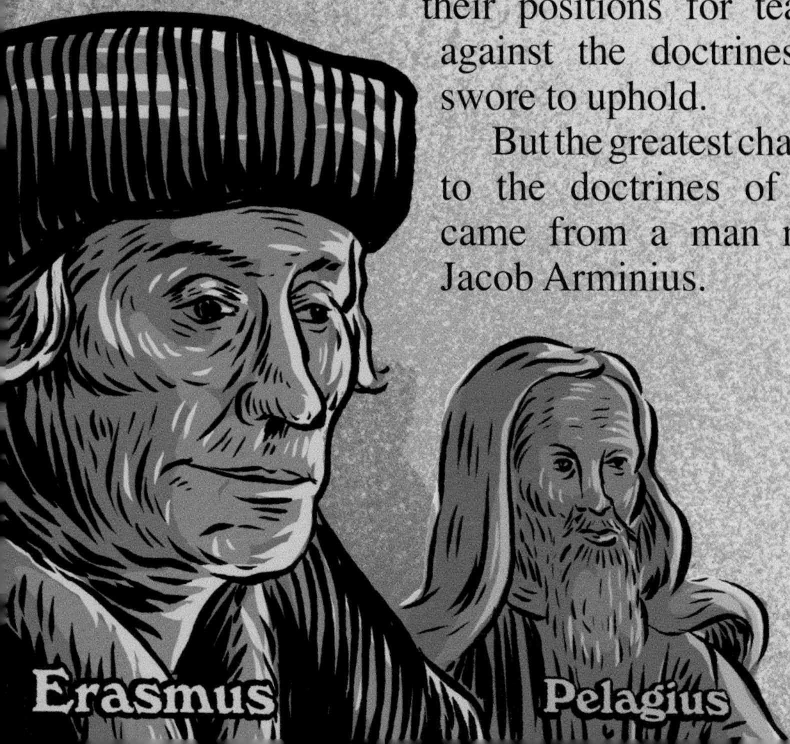

Erasmus

Pelagius

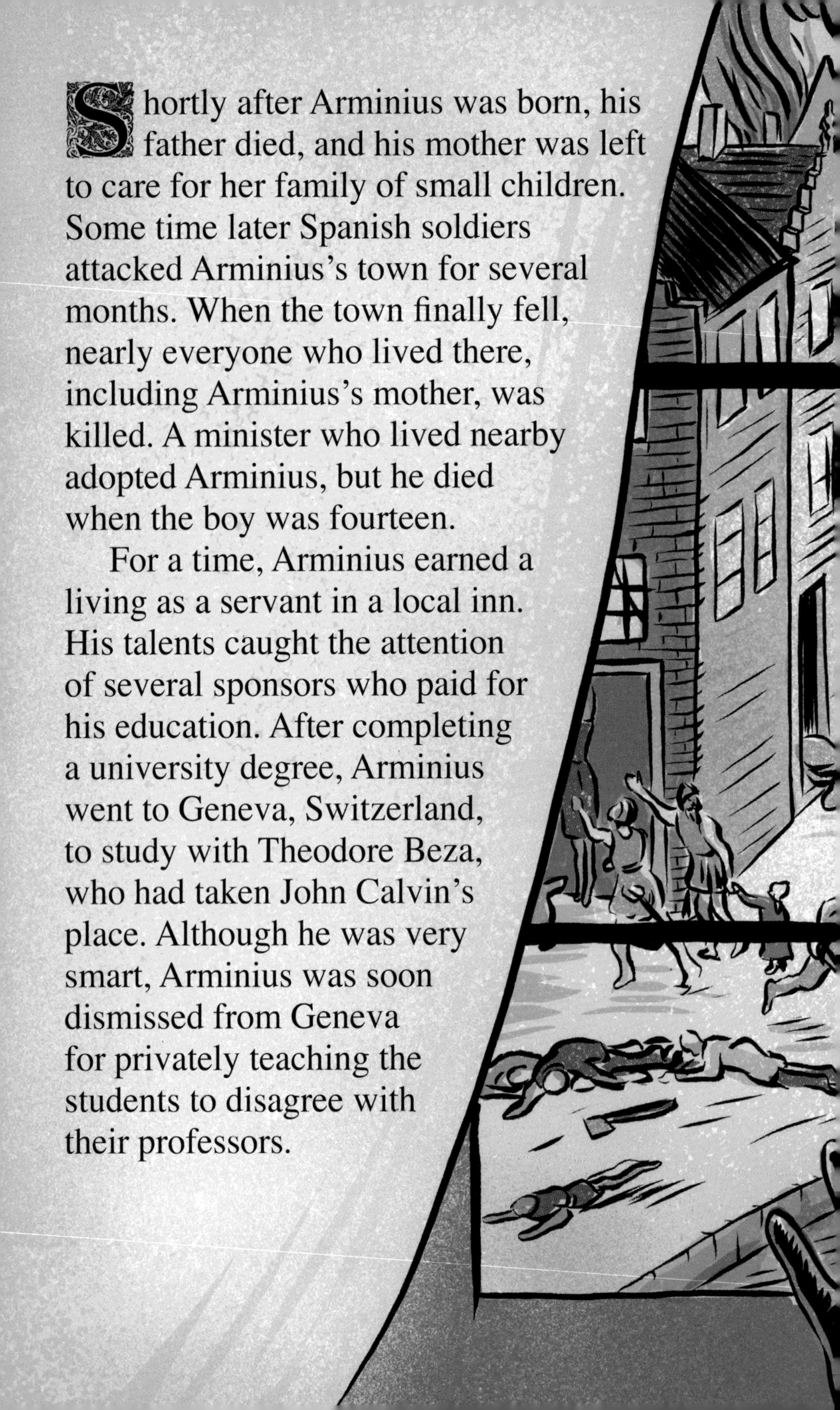

Shortly after Arminius was born, his father died, and his mother was left to care for her family of small children. Some time later Spanish soldiers attacked Arminius's town for several months. When the town finally fell, nearly everyone who lived there, including Arminius's mother, was killed. A minister who lived nearby adopted Arminius, but he died when the boy was fourteen.

For a time, Arminius earned a living as a servant in a local inn. His talents caught the attention of several sponsors who paid for his education. After completing a university degree, Arminius went to Geneva, Switzerland, to study with Theodore Beza, who had taken John Calvin's place. Although he was very smart, Arminius was soon dismissed from Geneva for privately teaching the students to disagree with their professors.

After leaving Geneva and becoming a popular minister in the Netherlands, Arminius began to preach against predestination, the teaching that God plans and guides all things. Instead of being disciplined for teaching against Scripture, Arminius was chosen to be a professor of religion! While he promised not to teach against Reformed doctrine, it soon became clear that Arminius taught one thing in public and another in private. Perhaps he was hoping to continue his secret teaching long enough to gain more support. But after attending a conference to discuss his views, he became ill and died in 1609.

That same year marked the beginning of a twelve-year truce in the war between the Dutch and the Spanish. During this time, the persecuted Pilgrim Fathers arrived in the city of Leiden, where Arminius would soon be buried. There they worshiped God freely until they left for America in 1620.

The year after Arminius died, his followers (called the Remonstrants) published a protest against the Reformed teachings of the Dutch church.

These Five Points of Arminianism stirred up disagreement among believers who had previously agreed with the Scriptures and the confessions on these issues.

The Remonstrance:
Or Five Points of Arminianism
I. God elects (or chooses to save) people simply because He knows ahead of time they will decide to repent and believe.
II. Christ died to save everyone, even though not everyone gets saved.
III. Sinners must cooperate with God in order to be saved.
IV. God's grace cannot overpower man's unbelief.
V. Christians can (we suspect) lose their salvation.

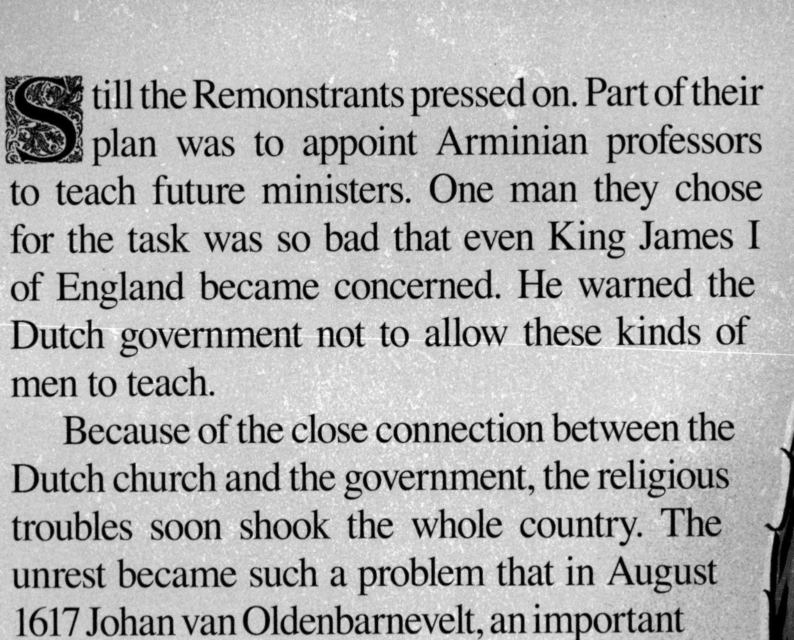

Still the Remonstrants pressed on. Part of their plan was to appoint Arminian professors to teach future ministers. One man they chose for the task was so bad that even King James I of England became concerned. He warned the Dutch government not to allow these kinds of men to teach.

Because of the close connection between the Dutch church and the government, the religious troubles soon shook the whole country. The unrest became such a problem that in August 1617 Johan van Oldenbarnevelt, an important Dutch leader, sent soldiers into the cities to restore order.

The churches needed a meeting called a "synod" to settle the disagreement. The problem was, in those days the government decided when synods could meet. This suited the Arminians since they saw the government as the head of the church. They also needed more time to win people to their side.

Around that time, King James I sent a letter from England strongly urging the Dutch government to call a synod. The new Prince of Orange, Maurice, gave the same advice. Since Maurice was the son of William the Silent and the leader of the Dutch revolt after his father's death, people greatly valued his opinion.

After much trouble from the Remonstrants, the decree was issued in 1618. Later that November the patriotic city of Dort would host a meeting to decide the religious future of the country. Before the start of the synod, the government declared a day of fasting and prayer to seek God's help.

On November 13, 1618, more than one hundred pastors, elders, professors, and government leaders from Holland, Germany, Switzerland, and England met in Dort until late spring of the next year. Each delegate swore an oath to conduct their business "using no human writing, but only the Word of God, which is an infallible rule of faith."

After arriving late, the Remonstrants tried to question the Reformed confessions rather than answer questions about their own views. Many of the people attending became frustrated and angry. At one point, the president of the meeting, John Bogerman, criticized the Arminians' actions with language so rough that even his friends felt uncomfortable. Unwilling to obey the rules of the synod, the Arminians were eventually dismissed. Synod proceeded without them.

When the last meeting ended, the synod had made several important decisions. One ruling would provide the Dutch churches with an improved Bible translation. The synod also gave instructions for worship services. The main songs used in church worship would be the 150 Psalms, as well as a few Scripture hymns. Parents were charged to train their children in the Lord at home as well as at school. Every Sunday afternoon ministers would preach the doctrines taught in the Heidelberg Catechism.

After much discussion, the synod rejected the Arminian protest and, without a single negative vote, issued five statements called "canons," which have become known as the five points of Calvinism. These

Canons of Dort became a statement of the Reformed church's beliefs, like the Belgic Confession and the Heidelberg Catechism. Together, these documents are called the Three Forms of Unity. Here is a summary of what the Canons of Dort said.

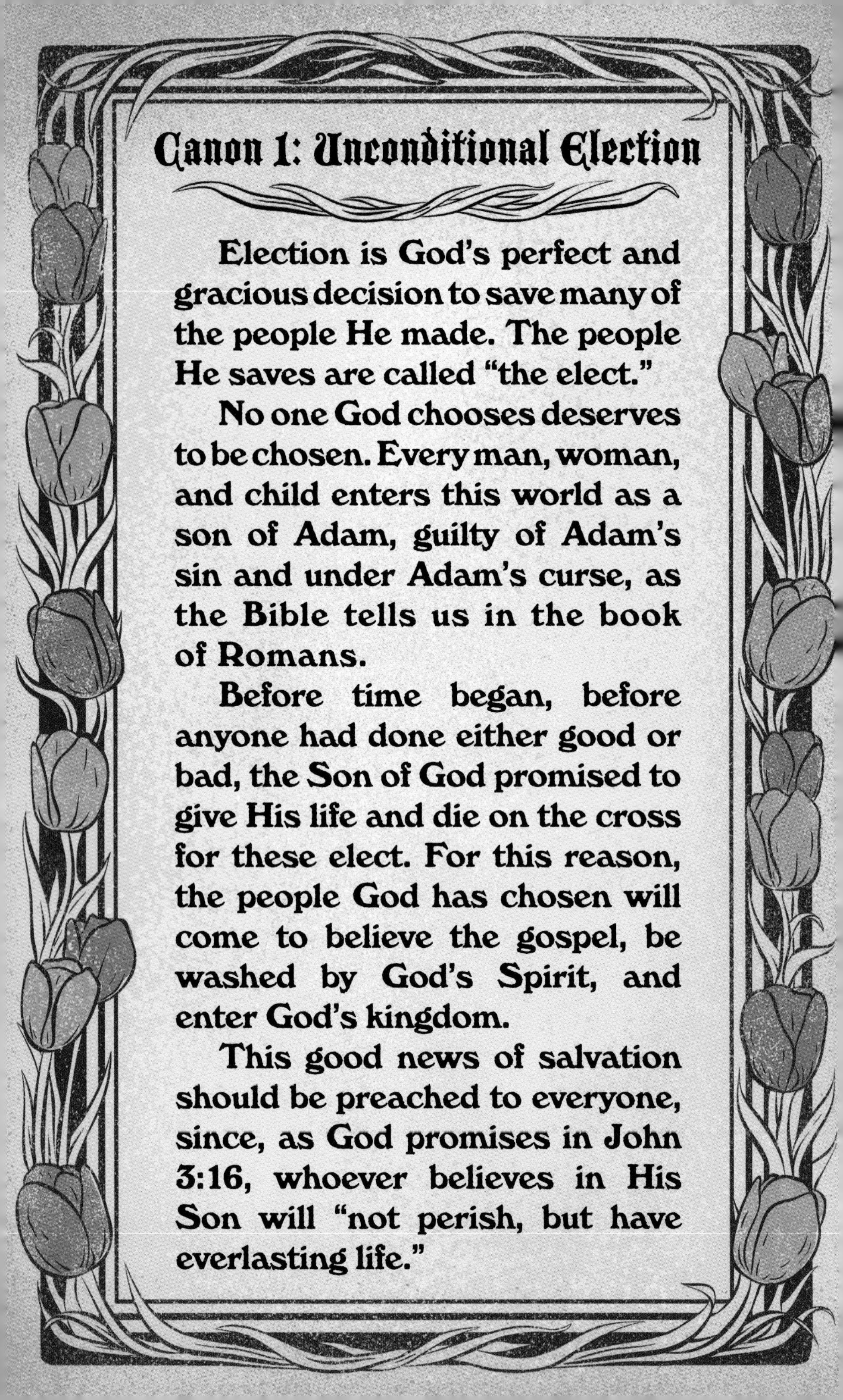

Canon 1: Unconditional Election

Election is God's perfect and gracious decision to save many of the people He made. The people He saves are called "the elect."

No one God chooses deserves to be chosen. Every man, woman, and child enters this world as a son of Adam, guilty of Adam's sin and under Adam's curse, as the Bible tells us in the book of Romans.

Before time began, before anyone had done either good or bad, the Son of God promised to give His life and die on the cross for these elect. For this reason, the people God has chosen will come to believe the gospel, be washed by God's Spirit, and enter God's kingdom.

This good news of salvation should be preached to everyone, since, as God promises in John 3:16, whoever believes in His Son will "not perish, but have everlasting life."

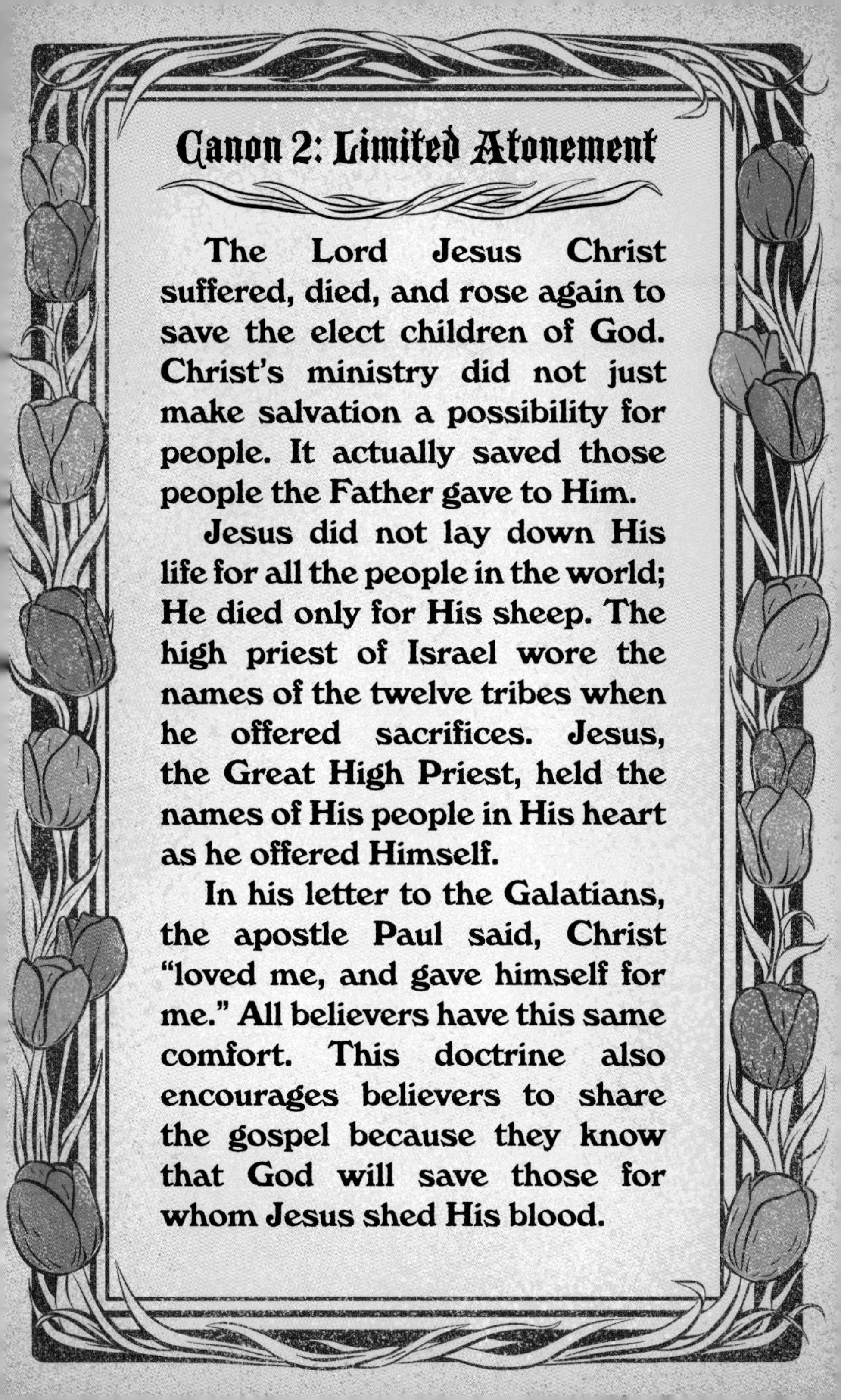

Canon 2: Limited Atonement

The Lord Jesus Christ suffered, died, and rose again to save the elect children of God. Christ's ministry did not just make salvation a possibility for people. It actually saved those people the Father gave to Him.

Jesus did not lay down His life for all the people in the world; He died only for His sheep. The high priest of Israel wore the names of the twelve tribes when he offered sacrifices. Jesus, the Great High Priest, held the names of His people in His heart as he offered Himself.

In his letter to the Galatians, the apostle Paul said, Christ "loved me, and gave himself for me." All believers have this same comfort. This doctrine also encourages believers to share the gospel because they know that God will save those for whom Jesus shed His blood.

Canons 3 & 4: Total Depravity and Irresistible Grace

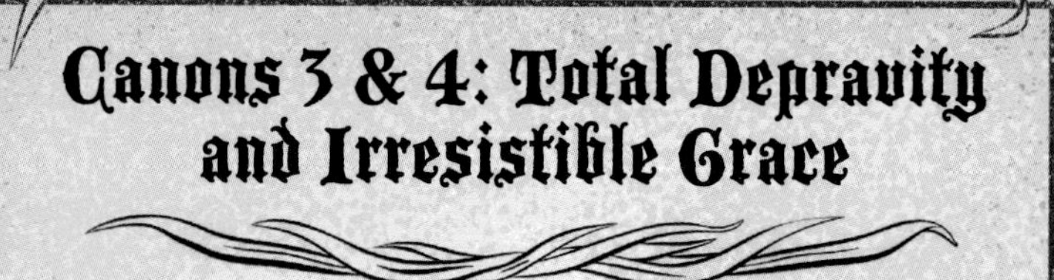

Although God created the first man, Adam, good and in His own image, Adam sinned. Because of Adam's sin, all his children are born in sin and are naturally set against God. In God's kindness, people in this life are not as bad as they could be, but every part of them has been infected by sin.

Because sinners can do nothing good, they naturally resist the goodness of God. To God's praise, the grace of salvation is so powerful that it wins over the hardest of chosen sinners. God's grace gives them a new heart to love Him and lovingly obey Him. God's grace shines light upon their minds so that they can understand the things of God. God's grace changes their desires, making them share the will of God.

Canon 5: Perseverance of the Saints

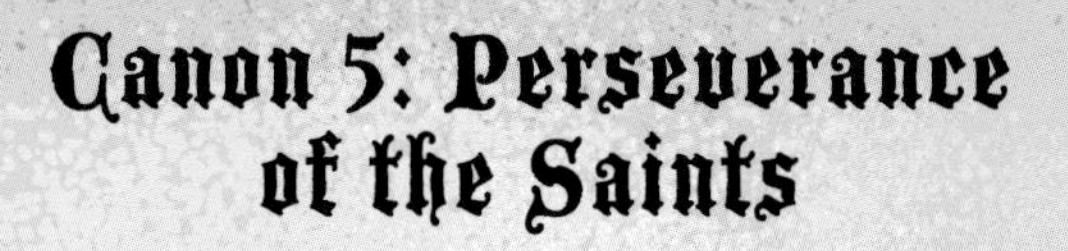

Believers can have confidence, as the apostle Paul tells us, that God began a good work in us, and He will continue working in us until He has finished at Jesus' return. Scripture does seriously warn believers not to harden their hearts and turn from the gospel. Sometimes believers sin terribly, like the apostle Peter, who denied Jesus three times. Such sin greatly offends God, harms others, and requires true repentance. Still, because God's plans can never be defeated, because Jesus pleads for us in heaven, and because the Holy Spirit is always with us, not one of God's children will be lost to hell. Because of this doctrine, believers can live joyfully to God's praise, thanking Him that He has kept them from slipping.

After the synod, Arminian gatherings were forbidden by law. Arminian ministers were let go from their positions; some were banished from the country. This seems harsh in our day, but it was rather mild back then. After the death of Maurice, Prince of Orange, in 1625, the Arminians were treated less severely, and many of the banished Arminian ministers were reappointed to their positions. Today, the Arminian view has become widely accepted in many churches. At the same time, many churches and believers are rediscovering the

Reformed faith. More and more people are coming to agree that this faith most greatly glorifies God and most greatly comforts believers.

Remembering the great synod, Bishop Hall, one of the English delegates and a man well respected for his godliness, said, "There is no place upon earth which I regard as so like heaven as the Synod of Dort." This synod remains one of the highlights in the struggle of God's people to maintain the glory of grace.

In recent years Calvinism has attracted new interest and in 2009 was one of *Time* magazine's top ten world-changing ideas. Broadly speaking, Calvinism is a world-and-life view that speaks to the head, heart, and hands with implications for church, family, vocation, government, and everything in between. The story of the Canons of Dort illustrates the close connection between doctrine and life and the need for a robust biblical faith that works even during the darkest of times (2 Tim. 3:10-11).

More narrowly conceived, Calvinism is the Reformed view of salvation. For many today the five points of Calvinism is a new idea. In reality, the Canons have been helping believers understand and express the gospel's simplicity to their children and others for almost four hundred years. As J. I. Packer suggests, Calvinism's five points can be boiled down to one: God saves sinners. First, the triune God alone provides the solution; man only contributes the problem. God the Father resolves, the Son redeems, and the Spirit renews. Second, in biblical salvation God saves to the uttermost (Heb. 7:25) as He links every aspect of our salvation into one unbreakable golden chain (Rom. 8:29–30). Third, the Scriptures ingloriously describe those whom God saves as dead in sins (Eph. 2:1) and worthy of eternal punishment (Rom. 6:23). In Packer's own words, "[God saves sinners] is the one point of Calvinistic soteriology which the 'five points' are concerned to establish and Arminianism…to deny: namely, that sinners do not save themselves in any sense at all, but that salvation, first and last, whole and entire, past, present and future, is of the Lord, to whom be glory forever; amen."

Sinners naturally struggle to accept the biblical gospel of salvation as a sovereign work of God. But Arminianism, while attempting to help, only makes the matter worse. Worst of all it robs God of the glory He alone deserves. Paul's approach is best: "O man, who art thou that repliest against God?" (Rom. 9:20–33). "For of him, and through him, and to him, are all things: to whom be glory for ever. Amen" (Rom. 11:36). When we and our children give God and His Word the final word, the glory of grace shines through.

For an excellent introduction to the background and theology of the Canons of Dort, see Cornelis Venema's *But for the Grace of God: An Exposition of the Canons of Dort* (Grand Rapids: Reformed Fellowship, 2011).